To the reader:

Welcome to the DK ELT Graded Readers.  different. They explore aspects of the worl geography, science … and a lot of other th different ways in which people live now, and lived in the past.

These DK ELT Graded Readers give you material for reading for information, and reading for pleasure. You are using your English to do something real. The illustrations will help you understand the text, and also help bring the Reader to life. There is a glossary to help you understand the special words for this topic. Listen to the cassette or CD as well, and you can really enter the world of the Olympic Games, the *Titanic*, or the Trojan War … and a lot more. Choose the topics that interest you, improve your English, and learn something … all at the same time.
Enjoy the series!

To the teacher:

This series provides varied reading practice at five levels of language difficulty, from elementary to FCE level:
BEGINNER
ELEMENTARY A
ELEMENTARY B
INTERMEDIATE
UPPER INTERMEDIATE
The language syllabus has been designed to suit the factual nature of the series, and includes a wider vocabulary range than is usual with ELT readers: language linked with the specific theme of each book is included and glossed. The language scheme, and ideas for exploiting the material (including the recorded material) both in and out of class are contained in the Teacher's Resource Book. We hope you and your students enjoy using this series.

LONDON, NEW YORK, MUNICH, PARIS,
MELBOURNE, DELHI

Originally published as Dorling Kindersley
Reader *Spies* in 2000 and adapted as an
ELT Graded Reader for
Dorling Kindersley by

studio cactus ©

13 SOUTHGATE STREET WINCHESTER HAMPSHIRE SO23 9DZ

Published in Great Britain by
Dorling Kindersley Limited
80 Strand, London WC2 0RL
A Penguin Company

2 4 6 8 10 9 7 5 3

Copyright © 2000
Dorling Kindersley Limited, London

A CIP catalogue record for this book is
available from the British Library.

ISBN 0-7513-2940-1
Colour reproduction by Colourscan, Singapore
Printed and bound in China by
L. Rex Printing Co., Ltd
Text film output by Chimera.trt, UK

The publisher would like to thank the following
for their kind permission to reproduce their photographs:
c=centre; t=top; b=below; l=left; r=right

AKG London: 8tl; Camera Press: 25tr, 25br, 25l; Corbis UK Ltd:
Bettmann 16bl; Robert Maas 39t; DK Picture Library: 18l, 29c,
31br, 34/35; Mary Evans Picture Library: 9c; Galaxy Picture
Library: Robin Scagell 41tr; Ronald Grant Archive: EON
Production 26tl, 26br; Robert Harding Picture Library: Dusty
Willison / International Stock 37t; Hulton Getty: 24tl, 27tr;
Military Picture Library: Robin Adshead 31tl; PA News Photo
Library: 17tr; Pictor International: 38b, 43br; Rex Features: 30b,
31tl, 46/47; The Sun 47tr; Tripett 45t; Science Photo Library:
NRSC Ltd 42t; Frank Spooner Pictures: 21c, 23br; Topham
Picturepoint: 10br, 19tr, 22c, 35tr, 40b, 44b.
Jacket: Corbis/Bettman: l; Camera Press: r

All other images © Dorling Kindersley.
For further information see: www.dkimages.com

see our complete catalogue at

www.dk.com

Contents

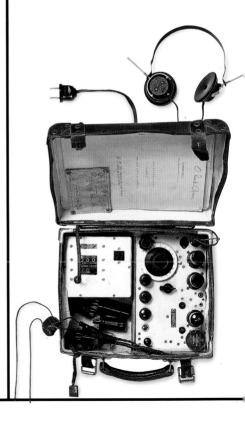

ELT Graded Readers

INTERMEDIATE

SPIES AND SPYING

Written by Mike Potter

Series Editor Susan Holden

A Dorling Kindersley Book

What do spies do?

He had waited a long time for this day. He had been observing the office building and everything in it for several weeks. But tonight he had a job to do and it had to be done quickly. He was in a dark office, in an enemy country. If he made a wrong move now, it would be the end of weeks of careful preparation – not to mention his career. He knew that he was breaking the law, and that if the police caught him, he might spend the rest of his life in prison. But he was a spy, and it is a spy's business to take risks.

He shone his torch around the room and soon found the safe. He knew that the plans would be in there. It wasn't difficult to break into the safe; he had done jobs like this before. He took out the precious sheets of paper and spread them on the desk. They were the designs for a new, top-secret missile. He shone his torch on the documents and photographed each sheet quickly, with a tiny camera. He returned the papers to the safe, leaving them exactly as he had found them, and silently left the building. No one had seen him – the mission had been a success!

This spy was helping to protect his country. The stolen plans would help scientists to defend their country from a new secret enemy weapon. But spies do many other jobs. Some work in their own country to protect it against attacks by terrorists. A few are secret killers. Many more guard their own country's secrets and protect them from enemy spies.

Ancient spies at work
There have been spies since ancient times. A Bible story tells how spies managed to enter the city of Jericho, a town in Jordan. Their leaders wanted to know how the enemy defended the city.

There are all sorts of reasons why people become spies. Some of them do it because they like excitement and are attracted by the idea of spending their life on dangerous missions in strange foreign countries or even in their own country. They find that living this secret and, sometimes, dangerous life can actually be enjoyable as well as exciting! But they also know that they will be well paid for the dangerous work that they do and the great risks that they have to take.

Others choose to spy against their own country because they disagree with their government. There are also cases of people who are forced to spy against their country. They may not want to become spies, but enemy agents threaten to blackmail them and reveal secrets about their lives that they do not wish other people to know.

Many people agree to become spies because they are concerned about what is happening in certain parts of the world. They think that the information that they manage to collect will help to protect the world and make it a safer place.

Businesses can provide plenty of work for spies, too. In the same way that countries try to find out their enemy's plans, companies need to find out what their competitors are doing. Industrial spying, or industrial espionage, is not only big business, it is also very sophisticated. When they steal secrets from their competitors, companies can make the same product at a lower price, or perhaps bring their product out onto the market earlier than their rivals. The equipment that is used in industrial espionage often uses the latest electronic technology, and the work can be just as dangerous as other kinds of spying.

Spies have always had to work in secret. But they do not always work on their own. They need to establish their own contacts, and develop ways to communicate secretly with other people. One of the oldest ways of passing on important messages is to write them in code. Codes turn messages into a sequence of letters that is impossible to understand. When the message is finished, it looks like nonsense, and most people would think that it doesn't mean anything at all. Only two people know that this is not the case: the person who sends the message and the person for whom it is written. Only they know how to read the secret code.

More than 2,000 years ago, the Roman Emperor, Julius Caesar, sent messages in code back to Rome when he was away from the city or about to fight an important battle. It was a very simple code, but it still prevented his enemies from finding out his secret plans. His code worked like this. He moved each letter forward three places in the alphabet. So A became D, B became E, and so on. When people received a message from FDHVDU, they knew that it came from Caesar himself!

Simple codes like this are easy to interpret, or crack, because each letter in the code represents the same letter of the real message.

A code is just like a lock – you can open it only with the right key! But, unlike Caesar's code, modern codes are very difficult to unlock, even though we now possess powerful computers and clever software.

Caesar was often successful in battles because of the accurate information that his spies collected about the enemy.

In many countries, spies are sentenced to death if the police or a secret service agent catches them. Sometimes, the situation becomes very dangerous and spies have to kill their opponents if they want to avoid capture. Other spies are trained specially as killers and are sent on deadly murder missions by their bosses.

Spies in 16th-century Venice had their own special weapons for these assassination missions. They used to kill their victims with daggers made of glass. When they attacked their victims, the glass blade entered into the body and then snapped off deep inside. The victim nearly always died from the wound that the knife had created, but the only clue that remained was a tiny cut on the skin.

The deadliest killers of all, however, were the 12th-century Japanese spies who were known as Ninjas – "invisible men". They were powerful fighters and completely fearless. They used to dress in black and climb over high walls and roofs or creep into people's houses to poison or stab their unsuspecting victims.

Modern murder
Spies still kill. A Bulgarian, Georgi Markov, was killed in London by a spy who used a gun hidden in an umbrella. The spy shot him with a poisoned pellet.

People used to say that no guard could stop a Ninja attack. If they agreed to undertake a mission, they would perform their task in the most rapid and efficient way possible. One clever Ninja hid for a long time in a small, dirty sewer, waiting for his victim to appear. Finally, his patience and the hours of discomfort were rewarded when his victim used the toilet above the sewer. The Ninja managed to kill him with a single thrust of his spear from below!

Wartime spies

When countries are at war, the work of spies is more important than ever. Spies try to find out everything that they can about the enemy army – how many soldiers it has, what sort of weapons it possesses and what plans it is preparing. Sometimes, they can gather the information by observation. They have to make friendships that could become dangerous if their real purpose was discovered. They also have to create situations where their informers will trust them and provide the information that they are looking for.

Spies in wartime must make sure that nobody is suspicious of them. They have to behave like normal people and lead a daily life that does not attract attention. At the same time, they have to develop ways of gathering the information that will help their army to overcome the enemy. So, unlike soldiers, spies do not wear uniforms. Instead, they live, dress and talk like the enemy that they are fighting against. Nobody must know their real identity, or the purpose of their mission. Spying is always a risky business. In wartime, it is even more risky than in peacetime. If they are caught, they will probably be tortured or executed without a trial.

John André, a British spy on a mission during the American War of Independence, didn't mind taking risks. In 1780, he heard that an American general, Benedict Arnold, would surrender his fort in exchange for a lot of money.

The two men arranged a secret meeting to discuss Arnold's proposal. Late at night, André climbed over the side of a ship and down a rope ladder into a small rowing boat. Wrapped in a large cloak, he stood at the front of the boat as it moved silently towards the beach inside enemy territory where the meeting was going to take place.

But things did not happen as they were planned. When André arrived at the place where they had agreed to meet, Arnold was not there. André was beginning to feel nervous. Was this a trap? Time was passing quickly. Soon, he would not be able to hide in the darkness any more. Day would begin to break and the risk of capture would become greater.

At last, as dawn was approaching, Arnold appeared and the two men had their meeting. But by now it was too late. The boat that was going to take André back to his ship had already left. He had waited too long. The only way to safety lay straight through the enemy lines. André would have to make his way back to British-held territory on foot.

It was too dangerous to risk this journey in daylight, so he found a place where he could hide safely, and waited for darkness to fall. Only then did he take the first steps on his dangerous journey to the safety of the British lines.

After walking for many hours, he saw a British camp in the distance. He was safe at last.

Then disaster struck! Three American soldiers appeared from nowhere and stopped him. They asked a lot of difficult questions and searched him thoroughly. They soon found secret papers, which he had in his boots. They knew that he could not be a soldier because he was not wearing a uniform. The only possible answer was that he was a British spy.

André suffered the fate of all spies who are caught by the enemy, and was shot without a trial, only a few metres away from the British lines and safety.

In World War II, both sides depended on spies to help them defeat the enemy. Britain trained spies to help the French after the German army had invaded France. Thanks to the support that British spies were able to give to the Resistance movement, the French could continue the struggle.

Sometimes trained spies were dropped into France by parachute at night, or left by boats on deserted beaches, far away from the enemy. All the spies wore disguises. They spoke French perfectly, wore French clothes and carried false passports, which hid their real identities from the Germans.

But they knew that every mission that they undertook was very dangerous. In the back of their minds was the fear that someone might reveal their true identity, or that they themselves might make a simple mistake that would put their mission in danger.

Sansom's safe secrets
Odette Sansom was a British spy in World War II. The Germans knew that she was a spy and finally caught her. She was badly tortured, but managed to remain silent. She did not reveal any secrets.

The Germans knew that there were a lot of enemy spies in France. They also knew about the French Resistance and how these spies were helping them. If they caught a spy, they did not show mercy. The punishment was to torture them until they gave information about their mission. Then they would be sent to prison or executed.

But the spies continued to help the French resistance fighters. Together they destroyed trains and bridges and helped to plan attacks on German bases. Radio operators sent secret messages to Britain about the movement of German troops and weapons. They also received secret instructions from coded messages in British radio broadcasts. The important information that these brave spies and the French resistance fighters managed to obtain, helped the Allied armies to liberate France in 1944.

German spies developed a top-secret weapon that they called Enigma. It was an amazing machine that was able to turn messages into very clever and complex codes. The Germans believed that nobody could crack these codes. It was, quite simply, impossible to do this, and they were very proud of what they had achieved. Enigma was the ultimate code machine! Nobody else possessed the technology or the skill to produce a similar machine. Indeed, British spies were unable to decipher any of the Enigma codes. But they had heard about the machine, and knew that they would have to crack these codes quickly, if the Allies were going to be able to win the war.

A German Enigma machine

Beware of the Bombe
While they were trying to crack the Enigma codes, scientists invented the world's first electronic computer. They called it Bombe, which was the name of a type of ice-cream that they used to eat!

The British government also realized the importance of Enigma. They contacted some of Britain's top scientists and asked them to help them to solve the Enigma problem! The scientists went to work at Bletchley Park, Britain's top-secret spy station. Their mission was to find the key that would unlock the secrets of the Enigma machine.

At first, they made little progress. Then, suddenly, the situation changed. They were in luck. The Allies had stolen an Enigma machine, and the Germans did not know that they had it! If the scientists could discover how the machine worked, they would then be able to crack the code systems that it created. They worked for months trying to find out how the codes were created. There were many disappointments and the work was slow and complex. But, finally, they got their reward. They found the key to the system.

The decoded messages were tremendously valuable, and helped Britain and the United States to discover vital enemy secrets.

"Peacetime" spies

In the 1950s, the world was not at war, but it was not really at peace, either. It was the time of the "Cold War", when the United States was frightened that communist countries might start another World War. Their answer to this threat was to build nuclear weapons of terrible power, much more powerful and destructive than those that they used against Japan at the end of World War II. They aimed these weapons at Russia and other communist countries. The communist countries were also afraid of the United States and the power of its nuclear weapons. So they built their own similar weapons and pointed these at the United States and Western Europe. A dangerous rivalry between the East and the West had begun.

Most countries supported either the United States or Russia. The Cold War was dividing the world into two blocks – those who supported the East and those who supported the West. This uneasy situation gave spying new importance. America's spy agency, the CIA, tried to discover how many nuclear weapons the Russians possessed and how powerful they were. Russia's spy agency, the KGB, sent spies on similar missions to the United States to find out the strength of its nuclear weapons. And both agencies tried to capture each other's spies.

A "mushroom" cloud after a nuclear test explosion.

When the United States built the first nuclear bombs in 1945, the KGB wanted to learn the secrets behind the creation of the world's most frightening and powerful weapon. They sent their best spies to the United States. Their mission was to find out all that they could about the atomic bomb.

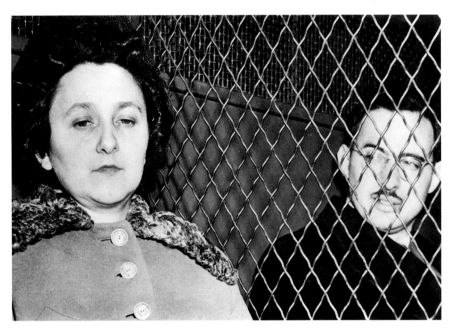

In 1950, the CIA arrested an American couple, Ethel and Julius Rosenberg. The CIA believed that they were KGB spies and that they had passed on vital secrets to the Russians. Ethel's brother worked on the development of the bomb and gave her information that soon found its way into Russian hands.

Ethel and her husband were tried in court. The court found them guilty of spying for the Russians and they were executed.

But the damage was already done. The Russians had all the information that they needed and had already produced their own nuclear bomb.

One of the worst moments in the Cold War was the incident that the world came to know as the "Cuban Missile Crisis". It happened in 1962. CIA spies in Cuba, a Caribbean island 150 kilometres from the United States, had noticed something strange. A lot of Russian "advisers" had arrived on the island. There was nothing too strange about that. But what interested the CIA spies was that all these advisers wore only two kinds of sports shirts. They guessed that they must be soldiers in disguise. When spy planes later spotted Russian nuclear missiles on the island, and took photographs of Russian ships near the coast of Cuba with suspicious cargoes on their decks, World War III nearly began.

Luckily, the Russians withdrew the missiles at the last moment and avoided a major confrontation with the United States.

Smoking is dangerous
The CIA felt that Cuba's leader, Fidel Castro, was a dangerous threat to the United States. They even plotted to murder him with an exploding cigar!

Philby and his mother.

Kim Philby was a very successful spy. He worked for Britain's spy service and helped it to catch Russian spies. Everybody respected Kim Philby; he was one of the best spies that the British had. The British even sent him to Washington, the capital city of the United States, to run courses for the CIA on how to catch spies. Then, in 1951, two of Philby's friends, who were also British spies, were caught spying for Russia. They managed to escape before agents could arrest them. Someone must have known that they were going to be arrested. Someone must have warned them. Was that person Kim Philby? "Me? No! Of course not!" he said.

But he wasn't telling the truth. Like his two friends, Philby was really spying for Russia. All three men were double agents. They pretended to work for one side, when they were secretly spying for the other side. Somehow, nobody at the time suspected that Philby was a double agent, or that he had anything to do with the convenient disappearance of his two friends. He was able to continue his treacherous and dangerous double act for another 12 years, right up to 1962. Then it was his turn to disappear!

He was in Beirut, in the Lebanon, at the time. Somehow, he found out that agents had been sent to arrest him. But he managed to disappear before they could find him. Six months later he reappeared. He was alive, and living in Russia – as a colonel in the KGB!

Kim Philby in Russia with his new Russian wife.

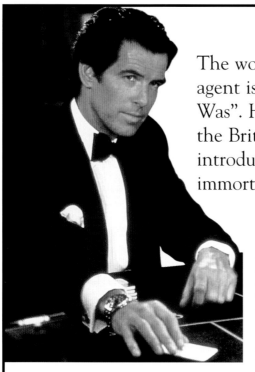

The world's most famous secret agent is the "Spy who Never Was". He is 007 and he works for the British Secret Service. He introduces himself with the immortal words, "My name is Bond, James Bond."

He is the perfect spy and the classic gentleman. His manners are perfect. His clothes are impeccable. They come from the best tailors and they never crease. He drives the most fantastic fast cars and he is licensed to kill. He has lots of enemies, and they are the most dangerous people in the world. Many of them just have one wish, and that is to dominate the world and everyone who lives in it. It is James Bond's job to make sure that they do not achieve their ambition. When he kills his enemies, he does it with great style. Nothing can be quite as dramatic, or explosive, as the end of a James Bond story!

Bond and friend escaping.

Poison pens
Like James Bond, the writer Ian Fleming loved clever and dangerous gadgets. He often carried a pen that could spray tear gas in an emergency.

Very often he finds himself in difficult and hair-raising situations, but he always manages to find a way to escape. An ejector seat in his car sends unwanted passengers flying through the sunroof. Missiles hidden inside his car destroy the helicopter that is relentlessly pursuing him. A helicopter, which he is able to store away in a suitcase, allows him to fly over an enemy's hideaway. Even his watch hides a razor-sharp blade to cut rope. There is no end to the inventions that are created to keep James Bond out of trouble!

Even though James Bond is not a real spy, the man who created him knew all about espionage. During World War II, Ian Fleming worked as a spy for the British navy. Many of his own adventures were even more amazing than Bond's. He had visited many of the exotic locations where the stories are set, and he based many of his fictional characters on people that he had actually met during the time that he worked as a British spy.

A spy's toolkit

All spies use clever tools and gadgets to do their work, and their job would be very difficult if they were not able to use them. Special cameras and video machines give them sharper eyes and help them to record vital information. Hidden microphones, which are so small that they cannot be seen, work like powerful ears. This means that valuable information can be collected far away from where a conversation is taking place. Like James Bond, real-life spies also depend on ingenious weapons and gadgets to help them to escape, if they are in a difficult situation or are caught.

Tools and clever inventions like these can make a spy's life much easier. But they can also make their life more difficult, and even get them into trouble. In many countries, it is forbidden to take photographs of planes, tanks, soldiers or military bases and equipment – even in peacetime. Cameras, recorders, microphones and other spying equipment could make people suspicious.

Deadly pencil
This looks like a normal pencil – but it isn't. It actually conceals a sharp and deadly dagger. Spies could use it to defend themselves against an enemy agent.

So the designers or inventors of these gadgets have to make them appear like something that an ordinary traveller might carry, like a calculator, a ballpoint pen, an alarm clock or even a credit card. Even the locks on an innocent-looking briefcase may hide a secret weapon.

An ordinary briefcase?

Spying is all about collecting information that can prove, for example, that someone is a traitor or that a country is developing a new weapon. Photos and videos help to provide the evidence. Spies use very special cameras and equipment. The equipment has to be small so that it can be hidden easily, but it also has to produce results of the highest possible quality. Magnifying lenses allow spies to photograph secret meetings from a long way away. At night, they use special lenses on their cameras that turn darkness into daylight. Spies have to be able to work 24 hours a day!

Soldiers wearing night-vision glasses that help them to see in the dark.

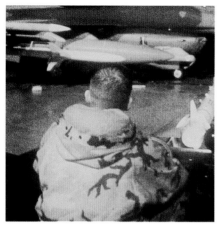

The view through a pair of night-vision lenses.

When an ordinary camera·might make a guard suspicious, but the situation requires a very high-quality picture, spies use tiny cameras that can be hidden in a matchbox and are very difficult to detect.

Spy cameras have been used for over 100 years. They used to be known as "detective cameras", because it was possible to hide them almost anywhere without raising suspicion. They were so small that they could be hidden in hats, watches – and even in a loaf of bread!

Super camera
During World War II, spies used a miniature camera, called a Minox, whenever they were sent on a mission.

Spies may have the most up-to-date cameras and possess important details of an enemy's secrets, but pictures and notes are useless if there is no way to get the information quickly to their bosses.

Today, this is not a big problem. Technology has come a long way from the early part of the 20th century, when spies were using birds as a secret airmail service during World War I. In those days, pigeons were specially trained to return to their home-base with letters and messages tied to their legs and feathers. Nowadays, spies can send information and photographs in a few minutes, by telephone, fax or by e-mail through a computer.

The situation rapidly improved with the invention of radio, when, for the first time, messages could be sent quickly and easily over long distances. There was no longer any need for the secret pigeon airmail service. Instead, it was possible to tap out messages in code on a clicking key, like the machines used by ships or to send telegrams from distant places.

Invisible ink
Spies can use lemon juice to write secret messages. The words disappear when the juice dries – and will reappear when the paper on which the message is written, is warmed up.

Each group of clicks represented a letter or a number. The message was sent immediately, not as speech, but as short and long bursts of radio waves. Although these radios made communication much easier, they also made it much more dangerous. Enemy agents listened for the messages. They did not always understand the meaning of the message, because it was written in code. But they were not really interested in the message. They wanted to catch the spy who was transmitting it, and had developed ways to trace the signals straight back to the radio set that had sent the message. Radio operators took tremendous risks, and many were captured.

British spies used this radio in World War II.

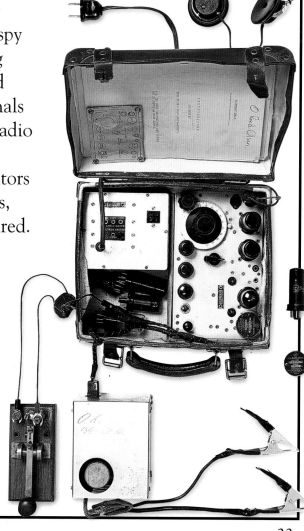

When you make a private telephone call, how many people hear it? Is it only you and the person who you are calling? Or is there another person listening, too?

It is quite easy to connect an extra phone or a tape recorder to a telephone line. This is called "phone tapping". Every time that the phone is used, the conversation is automatically transmitted to a special radio receiver. It is difficult to know if your phone is being tapped. Sometimes, people hear a strange click when they have a telephone conversation. This could mean that someone was tapping their phone and listening to their private conversations.

But telephone taps are not the only way to listen to a private conversation. Bugs – tiny radio sets and microphones – can also pick up and transmit speech. They can be hidden in any place in the house where two people may talk, in the kitchen, the dining room – even the bedroom, for example!

Pens that listen
This pen looks like any other, but it contains a tiny secret bug that can be used to listen to, and record, a private conversation.

Some spies dress up as telephone engineers or electricians, and install the bugs while they are pretending to do other work. Then they listen to conversations from outside the house!

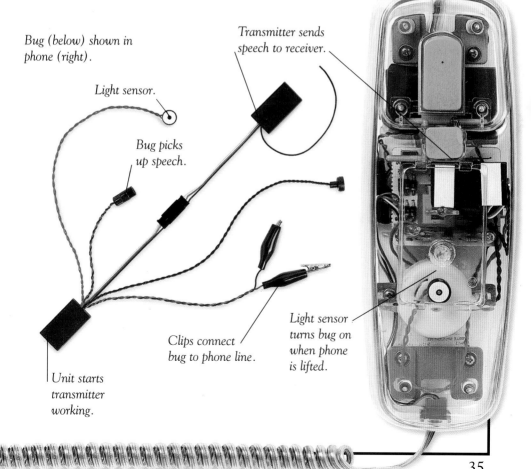

Bug (below) shown in phone (right).

Transmitter sends speech to receiver.

Light sensor.

Bug picks up speech.

Clips connect bug to phone line.

Light sensor turns bug on when phone is lifted.

Unit starts transmitter working.

Bugs work just like a radio, so it is easy to find out if your home contains one of the simpler types of bugs. All you have to do is to play some loud music in the room where you think that there may be a bug. Then take a radio and turn it on outside the house. When the radio is tuned to the same channel or frequency that the bug is using, you will hear the same music that you are playing in the room inside your home!

Other, more complex, bugs are much more difficult to find. That is because they do not always use the same frequency, and switch quickly between lots of frequencies. Some bugs even spread the sounds that the microphone picks up across a lot of frequencies. If you happen to tune in to one of these channels, you will pick up only a part of the sound that is being transmitted. Only the spies who installed the bug can hear the full message that it is sending.

Scramblers
A phone scrambler is a machine that keeps phone calls secret. Someone with a scrambler hears speech, but spies who are trying to listen to the conversation, will hear only a crackle.

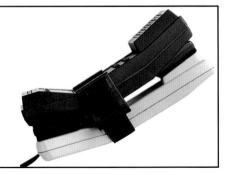

If you want to find and remove these bugs, you will need special tools to detect them.

Spies can attach a bug to any part of a telephone line.

It is much harder to find a telephone tap than a bug. Sometimes, if the job has been done in a hurry, you may be able to see where a spy has cut open the telephone wires indoors or somewhere nearby. But spies can fit a tap just about anywhere they wish. To find it you would have to search the whole line between the telephone and the telephone exchange, and that could take a very long time. If a tap is well fitted, and located in a part of the line that is difficult to reach, it will be almost impossible to find.

Modern spying

Today, of course, spies still continue to carry out their traditional work. But they are also starting to perform a new role. They are helping the police to fight crime. Of course, they are very well qualified for this job. They have learned some very special skills during their career. They know how to gather top-secret information. They have spent most of their lives dealing with difficult situations and they can defend themselves when they are in danger. They know how to disguise themselves so that they can move around in a way that doesn't make people suspicious of them. They also understand how to use complex electronic equipment, cameras and other gadgets. Above all, spies have learned how important it is to remain calm and patient. This is essential if you have to gather reliable information about suspected criminals.

Spies are very good at hiding in a crowd, sometimes in disguise.

Spies are helping the police to catch dangerous criminals.

These special skills can be very valuable to a country's police force. So some spies are now working very closely with the police in the fight against terrorists, drug smugglers and other dangerous criminals. Advances in telecommunications and electronic technology mean that they can use the latest equipment to help them to complete their mission safely and successfully. And, whoever they work for, spies now have a new and very powerful weapon – one that helps them to watch people and places secretly from the safety of space!

These powerful weapons are the satellites that travel high above the Earth. Satellites are a spy's best friend. While we lead our daily lives down here on Earth, the satellites are doing their work. They are busy taking millions of pictures of what is happening below them. These pictures are then transmitted to computers on the ground.

Spies can use the satellite pictures to discover important information. For example, during the 1991 Gulf War, satellite pictures made it possible for American spies to locate enemy tanks and soldiers.

Some of the photographs are so sharp that it is even possible to enlarge parts of the picture and count individual soldiers or missiles.

In the early days of space travel, satellite pictures were taken on negative film, just like the film that we use in our own cameras. When the roll was complete, it would fall back to Earth to be developed – a plane flying below would catch the film in mid-air before it hit the ground! Today's satellites use radio signals and computers to transmit their pictures to Earth. They can even receive instructions from a spy centre on Earth to take photographs of specific areas or cities.

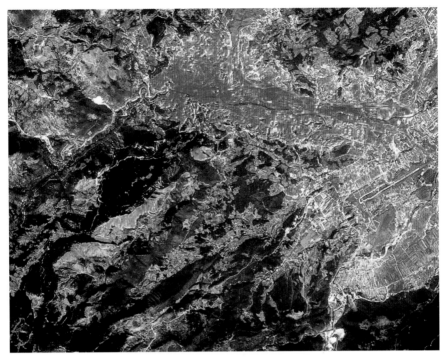

This satellite image shows buildings in pink. When the picture is enlarged, you can see smaller objects – even human beings.

The "spy's best friend" can help to collect information in all sorts of areas. It has been particularly useful in the fight against drug dealers. Satellites can help to locate the fields where the plants are grown that are used in the production of drugs. They can also identify aircraft and landing strips in the middle of the jungle, or the laboratories where the drugs are manufactured. This information helps spies to find the people who harvest and transport the drugs. When they have gathered enough evidence, the police can arrest the people who are involved in this illegal activity.

Spies also help police to follow and catch gangs who are involved in organized crime. They often go "undercover". They disappear from the place where they usually work, or become members of a gang that they are investigating. Only their bosses will know where they are at any time. Gradually, the members of the gang begin to trust them, and become more open about their plans and activities.

This is the time when the spy secretly starts to send information about the organization's plans and operations back to the police. For example, information on the methods that gangs use to obtain their weapons can be very useful to the police and can help them to defeat the illegal arms trade.

Spies in the CIA work closely with their police colleagues to help fight terrorism in the United States and other countries. For instance, their careful work helped to capture the group of terrorists who bombed New York's World Trade Center in 1993.

Terror tactics
Around the world, police and spies work together to try to stop terrorists planting deadly bombs like this one.

Although spies may be helping the police to defeat drug dealers and terrorism, they also have to make sure that their own secrets are safe. The recent case of Aldrich Ames provides an excellent example of how things can go wrong for a spy with the wrong kind of secrets.

Ames worked for the CIA. He had a very senior position in the organization and was responsible for catching Russian spies. In 1985, he was given the job of uncovering a double agent who had sold the name of every American spy in Russia to the KGB. But Ames seemed to make little progress in his search for the agent. After some time, people began to doubt whether he was the right man for the job. They just could not understand why he was unable to catch the traitor.

Aldrich Ames, when he was first arrested.

Aldrich Ames on his way to serving a life sentence in prison.

CIA chiefs also became suspicious of his lack of success and they started to follow him everywhere he went. They soon got a big surprise. Their cameras filmed the trusted agent as he stole secret papers and hid them in hollow trees. They also filmed the Russian spies who approached the same hollow trees and exchanged the papers for piles of money.

The reason why Aldrich Ames had been unable to catch the double agent was that he was the agent that everyone was looking for! His dealings with the Russians had made him rich. The American spies whose names he had revealed in order to become rich, were less lucky. They were all executed by the Russians.

Many of today's spies don't even have to leave home. Gone are the days when they had to travel on dangerous missions to foreign countries to gather their information. Now all they need is a computer and access to the Internet, which can link them to millions of other computers around the world.

Just like the suitcase radios and bugging devices that preceded them, the information that is transmitted by computers has to be protected from its enemies. China, for example, trained its top spies to use computer viruses to attack their enemies. Every two minutes, someone uses the Internet to try to connect to the Pentagon – the United States' war office. Most of these "attacks" are absolutely harmless, but not all of them. As soon as one threat is overcome, someone will find a new way to attack even the most protected computer systems.

Schoolboy spy
A "spy" who managed to find his way into the United States Air Force computers, was finally identified as Richard Price, a brilliant 16-year-old from Britain.

During the war in the former Yugoslavia, Serbian computer experts flooded NATO's computers with e-mail messages. They were trying to make the system crash, so that it could no longer operate effectively, and they nearly succeeded. NATO managed to repair the damage, but in future this kind of warfare on the Internet could do as much harm as bombs and bullets.

The rapid advances in information technology mean that the James Bonds of this world are having to learn plenty of new tricks!

Glossary

American War of Independence
The war (1776–1783) that North Americans fought to end British rule in their country.

to blackmail
To use an embarrassing secret to force someone to do something that they don't want to do.

broadcast
A radio programme when it is transmitted.

bugs
Tiny listening devices that allow spies in another place to hear conversations in the room where the bug is hidden.

CIA
Central Intelligence Agency, the spy agency of the USA.

code
A secret way to write a message and hide its meaning.

computer virus
A harmful program that spreads from one computer to another, and destroys information.

contact (noun)
A person you want to talk to or work with.

to crash
What happens when a computer receives too much information and is not able to function for a time.

disguise (noun)
Any way of changing a person's identity so that other people will not recognize them.

double agents
People who pretend to spy for one country while really spying for another country.

evidence
Facts which prove an idea or theory is correct.

gadget
A clever piece of mechanical equipment.

home-base
The place where someone or something begins a journey, or lives.

identity
Your personality, and who you are (name, age, family, etc.).

Internet
Worldwide network of computers used for trade, to provide information and to send messages (e-mail).

KGB
The spy agency of the Soviet Union (now Russia).

lock
The metal "teeth" that you can close with a key to stop people from opening a box, door or other object.